"IRENE & TANIS"

AND

"ZÉLIDE"

Borgo Press Books by VOLTAIRE

The Baron of Otranto and Other Plays
Candide: A Play in Five Acts
The Death of Caesar: A Play in Three Acts
Irene & Tanis and Zélide: Two Plays
Oedipus: A Play in Five Acts
Olympias and The Temple of Glory: Two Plays
Saul and David: A Play in Five Acts
Socrates: A Play in Three Acts
Two Voltairean Plays: The Triumvirate and Comedy at Ferney

"IRENE & TANIS" AND "ZÉLIDE"

TWO PLAYS

VOLTAIRE

Translated and Adapted by Frank J. Morlock

THE BORGO PRESS
MMXIII

"IRENE & TANIS" AND "ZÉLIDE"

Copyright © 2002, 2003, 2013 by Frank J. Morlock

FIRST EDITION

Published by Wildside Press LLC

www.wildsidebooks.com

DEDICATION

For My Dear Friend, Mike Lidsky

CONTENTS

IRENE 9
CAST OF CHARACTERS. 10
ACT I. 11
ACT II 30
ACT III 49
ACT IV 71
ACT V 90
TANIS AND ZÉLIDE 105
CAST OF CHARACTERS. 106
ACT I. 107
ACT II 120
ACT III 135
ACT IV 143
ACT V 156
ABOUT THE TRANSLATOR. 165

IRENE

CAST OF CHARACTERS

NICEPHORUS, Emperor of Constantinople

IRENE, wife of Nicephorus

ALEXIS COMNENUS, Prince of Greece

LEONCE, father of Irene

MEMNON, attaché to Prince Alexis

ZOE, favorite, follower of Irene

AN OFFICER

GUARDS

ACT I

The Action takes place in a room of the old Palace of Constantine.

IRENE:

What new change, what somber terror

Has separated us from the court and the emperor?

At the palace of seven towers a strange guard

In a dismal silence astonishes my sight here.

They've changed the court into a vast desert.

ZOE:

In the walls of Constantine, too often a fine day

Is followed by horrors of most funereal storm.

The court is no longer the noisy assembly

Of all our idle pleasures chained to one another.

Deceivers soothe unfortunate hearts.

You must retire from the importunate crowd.

Our Senators are assembled to reform the empire,

To ruin it, perhaps, and these fierce Muslims,

These vagabond Scyths, overrunning our fields,

Thousands of hidden enemies that we must yet fear,

Without doubt, at this moment are occupying Nicephorus.

IRENE:

Of his secret pains which he tries to dissemble,

I know the cause too well; it's going to overwhelm me.

I know with what suspicions his harsh jealousy

In his uneasiness outrages his spouse.

He hears in secret these detestable flatterers

Of a suspicious mind, detestable impostors,

Trafficking in lies and calumny

And covering virtue with their ignominy.

What a job for Caesar! And what sorrowful duties!

I pity him, I moan—it makes it twice as bad!

Ah! Why didn't I embrace that austere retreat

Where, after my marriage, my father shut himself up!

He fled the illusion of courts forever.

Hope which seduces us, which always deceives us,

Fear which freezes us, and cruel pain,

Which makes an eternal war on itself.

Why didn't I trample underfoot my funereal grandeur?

I mounted the throne in misfortune,

I am weeping before you my high destiny.

And I am weeping especially for this fatal memory

That my duty condemns, and makes me banish.

Here, the air you breathe poisons my life.

ZOE:

At least Nicephorus' somber jealousy

Hasn't manifested itself by indiscreet outbursts.

The shameful sentiment which torments him,

He hides from the vulgar, from his court, from himself.

He knows how to respect you, and perhaps he loves you.

You are seeking to nourish an unjust sorrow.

What are you afraid of?

IRENE:

Heaven, Alexis, and my heart.

ZOE:

But Alexis Comnenus in the fields of the Taurida,

Given entirely to glory and to duty which guides him,

Is serving the Emperor and you without disturbing you,

Faithful to his oaths to the point of avoiding you.

IRENE:

I know that this hero is seeking only glory.

I don't know how to pity myself for it.

ZOE:

He has through victory

Reaffirmed this long-tottering empire.

IRENE:

Ah! I've admired his dazzling exploits too much.

His distant glory has interested me too much.

Caesar will have surprised in the depth of my thought

Some indiscreet vows that I've been unable to hide,

And that a spouse, a master, may rightfully reproach.

Heaven created me for Alexis;

From ancient Caesars we received life,

And from our cradle, betrothed to each other,

It's in these same places we were united.

It's with Alexis I was raised.

The interest of state, this pretext invented

To betray his promise with impunity;

This terrifying phantom subjected my family;

My father sacrificed his daughter to his pride.

The crown of the Caesars was thought to hide my tears;

They decorated my pain in dazzling grandeur.

I had to extinguish, in my deep sorrow,

A passion more dear to me than the empire of the world.

I needed to tear myself away from the master of my heart.

Weeping, I dared to detach myself even from myself,

With the invincible power of religion,

Aiding my weakness in this guilty combat,

And learning to arm myself with this great aid,

I took the frightful oath of never loving.

I'll keep it. That word must make you grasp well enough

What rendings this heart must await.

My father, having been capable of exposing me to this storm,

Would have me learn to appease it by his virtues.

He left the court, he fled Nicephorus,

He abandons me to the prey of a world he abhors.

And I have only you alone to whom I can open

This weak and wounded heart that nothing can cure.

But they are opening the palace—I see Memnon appear.

(Enter Memnon.)

IRENE:

Well, can I see your master in freedom?

Memnon, can I, in my turn, be admitted today

Amongst the courtiers who approach him?

MEMNON:

Madame, I will admit that he wants, in your sight,

To hide the pains of his beaten soul.

I am not counted among the courtiers

Superbly confident of his secret plans:

Caesar shuts me from the entrance to his councils,

Commandant of his guard at the sacred gate,

A soldier forgotten by his old masters,

Relegated to my post like my warriors,

Only now I learned that the brave Comnenus

Long ago left the shores of Borystena,

That he's travelling towards Byzantium, and the worried Caesar

Listens all atremble to his assembled council.

IRENE:

Alexis, you say?

MEMNON:

He's scouring the Bosporus.

IRENE:

He could offend Nicephorus to this degree!

To return without his order!

MEMNON:

They are sure of it, and the court

Is alarmed, divided, and trembles at his return.

They say, he's broken the honorable slavery

In which the jealous Emperor retained his courage.

He's coming here to enjoy his honors and his rights.

That's all I could learn from these sudden rumors

Which are creating so many idle hopes in these parts,

And which, from mouth to mouth, are arming factions,

To prepare Byzantium for revolutions.

As for me, I know enough what role I must take,

What master I must follow, and who I must defend.

I am not consulting our ministers, our grandees,

Their hidden interests, their different factions,

Their false friendships, their indiscreet hates.

Attached without reserve to the pure blood of the Comnenus,

I am serving him, and especially in extremities,

Memnon will be faithful to the blood from which you come.

Time doesn't permit me to say more of it.

Allow me to fly back to where my duty engages me.

(Memnon leaves.)

IRENE:

What has he dared to tell me?

And what new danger is coming to afflict me again?

He didn't explain: I'm afraid of understanding him.

ZOE:

Memnon is simply a warrior prompt for all undertakings.

I know him: blood joins him to us sufficiently.

Exhaling his scorn against our courtiers,

He always detested their frivolous insolence,

Their animosities which divide Byzantium,

Their sad vanities that follow dishonor.

But his high mind especially hates the emperor.

Secretly, he's idolatrous of Alexis,

And if he's to be believed, Byzantium is a stage

Which will soon produce one of those reversals

Whose bloody spectacle enflames the universe.

You won't be astonished if his somber wrath

Escapes itself in speaking to you and depicts his character.

IRENE:

But Alexis is coming back—Caesar is irritated.

The surprised courtiers murmur, shocked.

The Senators convened in uncertain Byzantium,

Long weary of sovereign grandeur,

Trouble the whole empire with their divisions.

The whole populace is enflamed with the fire of factions.

What can I hope from Memnon's speech?

He commands a foreign guard at the palace.

Is he in secret, the confident of Alexis?

How I fear from Alexis' imprudent return,

The designs of the Senate, the delirium of the populace

And the burgeoning storm which threatens the empire!

How I fear myself in my just sorrow!

In secret I consult the trembling of my heart.

Perhaps it's preparing me for a terrible future.

In creating it, heaven made it very sensitive.

If Alexis ever, in this funereal place,

Betrays his oaths— What do I see? Just God!

(Enter Alexis.)

ALEXIS:

Deign to suffer my sight, and banish your fears.

I am not coming to trouble you with useless complaints,

A heart to which mine must sacrifice itself,

And to recall the times that we must forget.

Fates ravished from me sovereign grandeur.

It's done me further outrage; it deprived me of Irene.

In the submissive Orient my services rendered

Ought to have earned the treasures I lost;

But when they placed Nicephorus on the throne

Glory no longer spoke in my favor.

And having for support only our common ancestors,

I did not attempt anything which could make me approach them.

Today, Trebizond is delivered into our hands,

The Scythians repressed, Taurida conquered,

Are the rights which have finally recalled me towards you.

The reward for my labors was to be exiled!

Am I still by you? Don't you dare recognize

In my blood the blood which gave you birth?

IRENE:

Prince, what are you saying? In what time, in what places,

By this fatal return are you astonishing my eyes?

You know quite well what yoke holds me captive.

The eternal barrier raised between us,

Our duties, our oaths, and especially this law

Which doesn't permit you to show yourself to me.

To calm the unjust suspicion of Caesar,

It would have sufficed for you to avoid my presence.

You haven't foreseen what you are risking.

You are making me tremble; lord, you are ruining yourself.

ALEXIS:

If I feared for you, I would be more culpable,

My presence would be more suspicious.

What then! Am I in Byzantium? Is it you that I see?

Is this a jealous Sultan who holds you under his sway?

Are you in Greece a slave from Asia

That a despot, a barbarian purchased in Circassia,

That they throw in prison with cruel monsters,

Forever invisible to the rest of mortals?

Has Caesar changed in his somber crudity

The mind of the West and the morals of Greece?

IRENE:

From the day that Nicephorus received my faith,

You know quite well, everything changed for me.

ALEXIS:

Except my heart: destiny created it for Irene.

It braves the power and hate of Caesar.

It fears nothing but you! What! Your last subjects

Would have free access to their empress!

All mortals will enjoy the happiness of her sight!

Has Nicephorus forbidden in it me alone?

And am I a criminal to his jealous glance,

Since they made him Caesar, and he is your husband?

Puffed up with this august marriage

Does the excess of his happiness render him more unjust?

IRENE:

He is my sovereign.

ALEXIS:

No, he wasn't born

To despoil me of the treasure that was my destiny.

He isn't worthy of it and the blood of Comnenus

Wasn't transmitted to you to serve in his chains.

Let him govern, if he can, with his strict hands

This empire, formerly the Roman Empire,

That to the fields of Thrace, to the seas of Trebizond

Constantine transported to the misfortune of the world.

And that I've defended, less for him than for you.

Let him reign, if he must; I am not jealous to that degree.

I am following him for you alone; and never will my courage

Pardon him for your unworthy slavery.

You are hiding misfortunes of which your tears are

the guarantee;

And usurpers are always tyrants.

But if heaven is just, it will perhaps recall

That it owes the empire a less barbarous master.

IRENE:

Too idle regrets! I am a slave to my faith.

Lord, I've given it, it's no longer mine.

ALEXIS:

Ah! You owe it to me.

IRENE:

And it's up to you to believe

That I'm no longer to keep the memory of it.

I made those vows for you, and you are overwhelming me.

(Enter a guard.)

GUARD:

Lord, Caesar demands you.

ALEXIS:

He will see me; leave. (to Irene)

He will see me, Madame, such an interview

Must not worry your combative soul.

Don't fear for him; don't fear for me.

I know, at least, what I owe to his rank.

Return to your hearth, calm and reassured.

(Alexis leaves.)

IRENE:

With what a seizure my soul is penetrated!

How I feel weakness and horror at the same time!

Each word that he said to me filled me with terror.

What's he intend? Go, Zoe, direct that every hour

They secretly survey this sad dwelling,

These seven frightful towers, that, since Constantine,

Have seen the horrible fate of so many heroes.

Question Memnon, take pity on my fear.

ZOE:

I will go; I will observe this terrible enclosure.

But I am trembling for you; a suspicious master

Will perhaps condemn you and proscribe the two of you.

Among so many dangers what do you intend to do?

IRENE:

To keep my pure and simple word to my spouse,

To vanquish a fatal love, if its reignited fire

Is reborn in this previously enflamed heart.

To remain sovereign mistress of my feelings

If strength is possible to human weakness.

Not to fight in vain my duty and my fate;

And not to dishonor either my life or my death.

CURTAIN

ACT II

Same as in Act I.

MEMNON:

Yes, you are summoned; but Caesar is deliberating.

In his unease he consults, he delays,

Shut up with vile flatterers.

No question, the return of a hero has alarmed him.

But we still have time to speak to each other.

This room which leads to those of Nicephorus

Also leads to Irene's, and I command here.

Of all your partisans have no fear.

I have prepared them. If this iniquitous court

Dares to raise its despotic sword on you,

Count on your friends. You will see this pompous lot

Of proud slaves flee before them.

At the first motion our valiant escort

Are going to seize gates from the ramparts of the seven towers.

And the others, armed under clothes of peace,

Unknown to Caesar, are filling this palace.

Nicephorus fears you because he is offending you.

He places his confidence in this funereal castle.

There, in complete repose, with a word, with a blink of the eye,

He condemns to exile, to torture, to death.

He dares to count me among the mercenaries

Of his capricious frightful bloody ministers.

He's deceiving himself. Lord, what secret difficulty,

When I've prepared everything, seems to stop your steps?

ALEXIS:

Remorse. My heart must confess to you

Some fortunate exploits for which Europe is praising me,

My birth, my rank, the favor of the Senate,

All are shouting to me:

Come, show yourself to the state.

That voice excited me. Scorn urges me on.

My fatal passion dragged my youth.

I came to oppose glory to grandeur,

To share brotherhood and brave the emperor.

I arrive, and I foresee my new career.

Must I raise the standard of a rebel?

Shame is attached to this dangerous name.

Will I see myself carried beyond where I want to go?

MEMNON:

Shame! It's for you to serve under a master.

ALEXIS:

I dare to be his rival; I fear the name of traitor.

MEMNON:

Be his enemy in the field of honor.

Dispute the empire with him and be his conqueror.

ALEXIS:

Do you think that the Bosporus, and proud Thrace,

And these feckless Greeks will serve so much audacity?

I know that the estates are full of senators

Attached to my race, and whose hearts I have.

They are capable of supporting my bloody quarrel.

But the people?

MEMNON:

They love you; they are calling you to the throne.

Their courage is short-lived, they are dazzled by a great uproar.

A moment gives it birth; a moment destroys it.

I am inflaming this passion; and I dare tell you again

That I will answer to you for the hearts of all the empire.

Just appear, my prince, and you will make

The senate and the people instant conspirators.

In this bloody palace, abode of homicides,

Revolutions were always rapid.

Twenty times it sufficed to change the whole state

By the voice of a pontiff or the shout of a soldier.

These sudden changes are lightning bolts

Which in serene days burst over the earth.

The less they are foreseen, the less one can escape

Those devouring darts with which one feels oneself struck

We've seen these fugitive shades strike,

Phantom emperors raised on our shores,

Tumbling from the height of a throne into eternal oblivion,

Where their name in a moment is lost in shrouds.

It's time at Byzantium a man be recognized

Who's worthy of true Caesars and Rome's finest days.

Byzantium is offering to your hands sovereign power.

Those I've seen reign had only the will.

Carried into the hippodrome, they had only to appear,

Decorated by the purple and the scepter of a master.

At the temple of Sophia a priest consecrates them,

And Byzantium, suddenly on its knees, adores them.

They had less than you of friends and courage

They had less right; attempt the same work!

Gather up the debris of their broken scepters;

You will reign today, lord, if you dare.

ALEXIS:

Friend, you know me: I dare anything for Irene.

Alone she has banished me, alone she brought me back;

Alone over my still irresolute mind

Irene has kept her absolute power.

Nothing else is keeping me back;

They threaten her and I love her.

MEMNON:

I deceive myself, lord, or the emperor himself

Is coming to dictate his decisions to you in this retired place.

Will you still wait for him?

ALEXIS:

Yes, I will answer him.

MEMNON:

His guard is already appearing; it's confided to me.

If the studied hate of your enemy

Has conceived some secret designs against you,

We will serve under Comnenus, and we are Romans.

I am leaving you with him.

(Memnon withdraws to the back and places himself at the head of the guards.)

(Nicephorus enters followed by two officers.)

NICEPHORUS:

Prince, your presence

Has thrown a little challenge into my court.

On the shores of the Euxine Sea you've served me really well

But when Caesar commands, he must be obeyed.

You are being watched here with an attentive glance.

You are giving a dangerous example to the populace.

You mustn't appear within the walls of Constantine

Except on an express order emanating from my hand.

ALEXIS:

I didn't know it.— The Senate of the empire

Knows little of these laws you wish to prescribe.

I was able, without fail, to fulfill the will

Of an august and sacred body, and respected by you.

NICEPHORUS:

I shall protect it as long as it is faithful;

Be so, trust me; but since it is recalling you,

It is I who am sending you to the shores of the Euxine.

Leave this moment the walls of Constantine.

You have no further excuse; and towards the Bosporus

The day star which shines will see you off again.

You are no more for me anything but a subject in revolt.

You will not be so with impunity.

That's what Caesar intended to tell you.

ALEXIS:

The great by whose acclamation you were given the empire

Made me the first person in the state after you,

Lord, could bend this violent wrath.

They know my name, my rank, and my service,

And you yourself, with them, will give me justice.

You will let me live within these sacred walls

That my arm has delivered from your enemies.

You will not separate me from an inviolable right

That the law of the State only ravishes from the guilty.

NICEPHORUS:

You dare to pretend to it?

ALEXIS:

A simple citizen

Would dare it, is owed it, and my right and his

Is that of all mortals; fate which outrages me

Has not marked my face with the seal of slavery.

It's the right of Alexis; and I believe it is due

To the blood which has been shed for you many times,

To the blood whose valor has paid your glory,

And which can equal without increasing very much

The blood of Nicephorus, formerly unknown,

Today reaching the rank of my ancestors.

NICEPHORUS:

I know your race, and what's more your arrogance.

For the last time, beware my vengeance.

You will not obey me?

ALEXIS:

No, lord.

NICEPHORUS:

That's enough. (calling Memnon to him by a gesture, he gives him a note in the back)

You who obey me, serve the empire, and me.

(Nicephorus leaves.)

MEMNON:

Me, serve Nicephorus!

ALEXIS:

(after having observed first the place where he finds himself)

First, I must learn

What this note you were just given says.

MEMNON:

Look.

ALEXIS:

(after having calmly read a part of the note)

In his council the order was taken!

And I should have been made to wait for this atrocity!

He flatters himself that as master he condemned Comnenus.

He signed my death.

MEMNON:

He signed his.

Surrounded by slaves, this shadowy tyrant,

This blind despot thought me cowardly like them.

How this palace has produced the habit

And the barbarism of servitude!

So long as our shaky Caesars on their frightful throne

Think to reign without laws and speak like sultans!

But get it over with, read this pitiless order.

ALEXIS:

(rereading) This despot is more culpable than I thought.

Irene, prisoner! Is it really true, Memnon?

MEMNON:

For the great, their tomb is near the prison.

ALEXIS:

O heaven! Is Irene informed of your projects?

MEMNON:

She can suspect it, both the cause and the result.

The rest is unknown.

ALEXIS:

Let's avoid afflicting her;

And especially, dear friend, let's hide her danger from her.

The enterprise must soon be discovered.

But that's when my victory or my ruin will be known.

MEMNON:

Our friends are joined to these brave soldiers.

ALEXIS:

Are they ready to march?

MEMNON:

Lord, don't doubt it.

At this moment their troop is going to open a passage.

Believe that friendship, zeal, and courage

Are of a greater service in these urgent perils

Than all the battalions paid by tyrants.

I see them advancing toward the sacred gate.

The Emperor himself is going to defend the entrance.

I already hear the shouts of the roused populace.

ALEXIS:

We have only a moment; I reign or I perish.

Fate is cast. Let's forestall Nicephorus. (to soldiers)

Come, brave friends, with whom my destiny honors

me,

You've fought under Memnon and under me,

Fight for Irene, and avenge her virtue.

Irene belongs to me, I cannot take her back

Except under waves of blood and under walls of ashes.

Let's march without hesitation.

(Enter Irene.)

IRENE:

Where are you rushing? O heaven!

Alexis! Stop: what are you doing? Cruel one!

Remain: surrender to my legitimate concerns.

Avoid your ruin, spare yourself crimes.

I'm frozen with terror at the very name of revolt.

It speaks to me of blood which is going to pour out for me.

I'm no longer permitted, in my mute sorrow,

To devour my tears in the depth of my retreat.

My father, at this moment, excited by the populace,

Is heading towards the palace which he deserted.

The pontiff is following him, and in his ministry

Attesting to the wrath of God whom they are outraging.

They are both seeking you in these pressing dangers.

Lord, hear them.

ALEXIS:

Irene, there isn't time.

The quarrel is too great, it is too urgent.

I will listen to them when you've been avenged.

(Exit Alexis, Memnon, and their friends.)

IRENE:

He's fleeing me! What will become of me?

O heaven! And what a moment!

My husband is going to perish or strike down my lover!

I am throwing myself in your arms, O God who caused my birth!

You, who made my fate, who gave me for a master

A respectable mortal who received my word;

That I ought to love, if possible, despite myself!

I heard my reason, but my unfaithful soul,

Wanting to obey you, rose against it.

Lead my steps, sustain this weak reason,

Give life to this heart dying by its poison.

Restore peace to the empire as well as to myself.

Preserve my husband: order me to love him.

The heart depends on you: human misfortunes

Are the vile instruments of your divine hands.

In this terrible disorder watch over Nicephorus.

And when my despair implores you for my spouse,

If other feelings are still permitted to me,

God, who knows how to pardon, watch over Alexis.

ZOE:

(returning) They are in our hands; return.

IRENE:

And my father?

ZOE:

He's coming;

He's parting the waves of people, and the fearful crowd

Of women, old men, children, who in their arms

Push to heaven cries that heaven does not hear.

The holy pontiff, with a useful aid

To the wounded, to the dying, in vain is giving asylum.

The fierce conquerors are sacrificing on the altar

The escaped vanquished from this cruel battle.

Don't expose yourself to this populace in fury.

I see Byzantium falling, and the fatherland perishing,

That our trembling hands cannot revive

But you can ruin yourself trying to save them.

At least await some news of the battle.

IRENE:

No, Zoe, heaven wants me to fall with her.

No, I must not live in our burning walls,

In the midst of tombs that my hands have created.

CURTAIN

ACT III

Same as in Act I.

ZOE:

Your unique role, madame, was to await

The irrevocable decree that destiny is going to render.

In the ranks of soldiers, a Scythian would have been able

To call on danger and to seek death;

Under the rigorous heavens of their savage climate,

The harshness of morals has produced these customs.

Nature has established other laws for us.

Let's submit ourselves to fate, and whatever may be its choice

Let's accept, if need be, the master that it gives us.

By birth, Alexis touched the crown,

His valor deserved it; he brings to this battle

That great heart and that arm which defended the state.

Especially in his favor he has the public voice.

It detests a tyrannical power

As much as it cherishes an oppressed hero.

He'll conquer because he is loved.

IRENE:

Eh! What's the use of being loved?

You are just more unfortunate. I feel that myself too much.

I fear discovering if it is true that I love him,

To question my heart and only dare

To ask what is the result of the battle.

How much blood was spilled, who are the victims,

How many crimes I have gathered together in this palace?

They are all my work.

ZOE:

To your just sorrows

Do you want to add the terrors of remorse?

Your father left his holy retreat

Where his sad virtue is hidden unknown.

It's for you he's viewing these dangerous mortals again,

Whose approach he fled to the shadow of altars.

He was dead to the world; he's returning to it for his daughter,

In this same palace where his family reigned.

You will find consolation in him

That destiny is refusing to your affliction.

Throw yourself into his arms.

IRENE:

Will he find me worthy of him?

Have I deserved what this effort reveals,

Bringing him to his daughter in this cruel abode,

Where for me he affronts the horrors of the court?

(Leonce enters.)

Is it you who contemplates my despair in these parts?

Support of the unfortunate, my father, my example.

What! You are leaving the abode of peace for me!

Alas! What crimes have you seen in it?

LEONCE:

The walls of Constantine are a field of carnage.

Thanks to heaven, I am unaware what astonishing storm,

What court interests, what factions,

Have suddenly given birth to these desolations.

They've told me that Alexis, armed against his master,

Has dared to appear with conspirators.

One said that he received the death that he deserved.

The other that his emperor was fleeing before him.

They believe Caesar is wounded; the battle is still going on

From the gates of the seven towers

To the shores of the Bosporus.

Tumult, death, and crime are in these parts.

I am coming to snatch you from these odious walls.

If you have lost in this funereal battle

An empire, a husband, let virtue remain to you.

I have seen too many Caesars in this bloody abode

From this throne degraded overturned one after the other

Only that of God, my daughter, is unshakeable.

IRENE:

They're coming to complete the horror which overwhelms me.

And here are the warriors who are announcing my fate to me.

(Enter Memnon and soldiers.)

MEMNON:

He's no longer tyrant, it's done, he's dead.

I saw it. It was in vain that repressing his rage,

While holding under his feet this fatal adversary,

Alexis, his conqueror, wished to spare him.

The populace was bathing in his burning blood.
   (coming forward)

Madame, Alexis reigns, everything conspires with
   my wishes.

A single day has changed the fate of the empire.

While Victory on our happy ramparts

Raises with its hands the throne of the Caesars,

While Alexis is restoring peace, he is sending me to
   your feet

To interpret and witness the public joy.

Forgive, if his mouth at this same moment

Doesn't announce this great event,

If the effort of stopping the blood and carnage

Still busies his courage far from your eyes;

If he's unable to bring to your sacred knees

The laurels that his hands have gathered for you.

I am flying to the Hippodrome, to the Temple of Sophia,

To the assembled estates to save the country.

We are all going to name with the holy name of emperor

The hero of Byzantium and its liberator.

(He leaves.)

IRENE:

What ought I to do? O God!

LEONCE:

Believe a father and follow him.

In this abode of blood you cannot live

Without rendering yourself execrable to posterity.

I know that Nicephorus was too brutal;

But he was your spouse: respect his memory,

The duties of a wife, and especially your glory.

I will not tell you that it is appropriate for you

To avenge by blood, the blood of your spouse.

That's only a barbarous right, a power that's founded

On the false prejudices of false worldly honor.

But it's a frightful crime, which cannot be expiated

By being in communication with the murderer.

Contemplate your condition: on one side is presented

An audacious youth whose bloody hand

Has just sacrificed a master to his ambition.

On the other is duty and religion,

True honor, virtue, God himself.

I won't speak to you of a father who loves you.

It's you that I want to believe in; listen to your heart.

IRENE:

I'm listening to your advice: lord, they are just.

They are sacred. I know that a respectable custom

Prescribes solitude to my fatal widowhood.

I ought to seek peace in your holy refuge,

For in this bloody palace, I've never known it.

I have too great a need to flee, both this world that I love

And its horrible prestige—and flee even from myself.

LEONCE:

Come then, dear support of my decrepitude.

With me forget all that I have left

In the breast of the retreat; believe there is still

Consolation for an unquiet soul.

There I found that peace that you are searching for in vain.

I will lead you there, I know the way.

I am going to prepare everything— Swear to your father,

By the God who leads me, and whose eye enlightens you,

That you will fulfill, in these sad ramparts,

The duties imposed on the widows of Caesars.

IRENE:

It's true these duties can seem austere,

But if they are strict, they are necessary to me.

LEONCE:

Let Alexis be forever forgotten by us.

IRENE:

If I must forget him, why speak to me of him?

I know that I ought to have asked you for mercy

These bonds you are offering me and that I must embrace.

After the frightful storm that I've just endured

In the port with you all must be forgotten.

I've hated this palace, where a flattering court

Offered me vain pleasures, and thought me happy.

If it's tainted with blood, I ought to detest it.

Eh! What regret, lord, ought I to have to quit it?

God has commanded it to me through the voice of a father.

I owe him obedience and I am going to satisfy you.

I am placing in your hands a solemn oath.

I am descending from this throne and I am marching to the altar.

LEONCE:

Goodbye: remember this terrible oath.

(Leonce leaves.)

ZOE:

What is this new yoke that on your sensitive heart

A father imposes anew on this terrifying day?

IRENE:

Yes, I intend to fulfill this strict oath.

Yes, I intend to consummate my fatal sacrifice.

I am changing prisons, I'm changing tortures.

You, who, always present to my diverse torments

To the trouble of my heart, to the weight of my fetters

Shared so many troubles and secret sorrows,

Will you dare to follow me to the depth of these retreats

Where my unhappy days are going to be enshrouded?

ZOE:

Mine are at all time subjected to yours.

I see that our sex is born for slavery.

On the throne, at all times, that was your share.

Those moments, so brilliant, so short, so deceitful,

That they called your fine days were lengthy misfortunes.

Sovereign in name, you served a master.

And when you were free, and that you ought to be,

The dangerous weight of your dignity

Instantly plunged you back into captivity!

Customs, laws, public opinion,

All hold you under a tyrannic yoke.

IRENE:

I will wear my chain—I'm no longer permitted

To dare to interest myself in the plans of Alexis.

I cannot breathe the air that he breathes.

Let him be the savior of the empire to other eyes,

Let them cherish in him the greatest of Caesars,

He is only a criminal to my sad sight.

He is only a parricide, and my soul is constrained

To drive Alexis from my sad thoughts.

If, in the solitude that I am going to enclose myself in,

I recollect to myself that Alexis was lovable,

That he was a hero—I will be very culpable.

Go, my dear Zoe, go hurry my departure,

Save me from an abode that I have left too late.

I am going to find the pontiff and my father immediately.

And I am striding fearlessly towards

The pure day which enlightens me. (seeing Alexis)

Heaven!

(Enter Alexis and guards; the guards retire after having placed a trophy at Irene's feet.)

ALEXIS:

On this day of terror, I am placing at your feet

All that I owe you, an empire and my heart.

I wasn't fighting over this funereal empire;

It was nothing without you: celestial justice

Ought to despoil unworthy sovereigns

Only to reestablish it with your august hands.

Reign, since I reign, and let this day begin

My happiness, and yours and that of Byzantium.

IRENE:

What a horrifying joy! Ah! prince! You are forgetting

That you are covered with the blood of my husband?

ALEXIS:

Yes! I intend to efface his memory from the earth,

So that his name will be lost in the dazzle of my glory.

That in its happiness the Roman Empire

Will be unaware if he ever reigned, if he ever was.

I know that these great blows, the first day,

Are murmuring through astonished Asia and Greece.

It gives rise to censors, to rivals.

Soon, accustomed to its new masters

They will end by loving their established power.

Let them know a governor, madam, and everything's forgotten.

After a few moments of a just severity

That the public interest demands of a conqueror,

You will bring back the fine times in which happy Livia

Made the submissive earth adore Augustus.

IRENE:

Alexis! Alexis! We are only abusing ourselves.

Crime and death have marched behind our steps.

Blood shrieks: it rises, it demands justice.

Murderer of Caesar, am I your accomplice?

ALEXIS:

That blood saved yours and you are punishing me for it?

Who? Me? I'm guilty in your offended eyes!

A jealous despot, a pitiless master,

Thanks only to the name of husband is respectable for you!

His days were sacred to you! And your defender

Was only a rebel, then, only a ravisher!

When I dared to defend you against your tyrant

Ought I to have expected your ingratitude?

IRENE:

I wasn't ungrateful: one day you will learn

The unhappy battles of my torn feelings.

You will pity a woman in whom, from her infancy,

Her heart and her relatives formed the hope

Of spending the unalterable course of her life

Under the laws, under the eyes of a hero of our time.

You will then know what it cost, what she sacrificed,

The happiness of her life to her sacred duties.

ALEXIS:

What! You are weeping, Irene! And you are abandoning me!

IRENE:

We are condemned to flee each other forever.

ALEXIS:

Eh! Who then condemns us? A fanatic law,

A senseless respect for ancient custom

Embraced by a populace in love with errors,

Scorned by Caesars and especially by conquerors!

IRENE:

Nicephorus holds me enslaved from the tomb.

And his death separates us yet further than his life.

ALEXIS:

Dear and fatal Irene, arbitress of my fate,

You are avenging Nicephorus and giving death to me.

IRENE:

Live, reign without me, make the empire happy.

Fate is seconding you: it intends that another expire.

ALEXIS:

And you deign to speak with so much goodness,

And you are being stubborn with so much cruelty!

What you are offering me is worse than hate and wrath.

Will you be to yourself even totally contrary?

I see, a father is constraining you to flee me.

To whom else would you have promised to betray yourself?

IRENE:

To myself, Alexis.

ALEXIS:

No, I cannot believe it.

You didn't seek this frightful victory,

You aren't renouncing the blood you come from.

To your submissive subjects, to your properties,

To go shut this adored head

In the obscure redoubt of a holy prison.

Your father is deceiving you: an imprudent error,

After having seduced him, is seducing your heart.

It's a new tyrant whose hand is oppressing you.

He's sacrificed himself and is making you his victim.

Has he fled humans so as to torment them?

Is he coming out of his tomb to persecute us?

More cruel towards you than even Nicephorus,

Does he want to murder a daughter that he loves?

I am rushing to him, madame, and I don't intend

That he give laws against me in my realm.

If he scorns the court and his heart abhors it,

I won't suffer that he still govern it.

And that the imprudent severity of his mind

Persecute his blood, his master, and his avenger.

(Enter Zoe.)

ZOE:

Madame, they are waiting for you; Leonce, your father,

The minister of God who rules the sanctuary,

Are ready to escort you, alas, according to your wishes,

To this august asylum—happy or unhappy.

IRENE:

Everything is ready: I follow you.

ALEXIS:

And as for me, I am forestalling you.

I am going to repress the insolence of these ingrates.

To assure myself in their eyes of the reward of my labors

And twice in one day to conquer all my rivals.

(Exit all but Irene.)

IRENE:

What's going to become of me? How shall I escape

This horrible precipice, this redoubtable trap,

Into which my distracted steps are leading me despite myself?

My lover has killed my husband and my king,

And on his bloody corpse this raging hand

Dares to ignite for me the torch of marriage!

He intends that this mouth on the steps of the altar

Swear an eternal love to his murderer!

Yes, great God, I love him; and my distracted soul

Is still intoxicated with this fatal poison.

What do you want from me, dangerous Alexis?

Lover that I cherish, lover that I am abandoning,

Are you forcing me into crime and do you still intend

To be more my tyrant than Nicephorus was?

CURTAIN

ACT IV

Same as in Act I.

ZOE:

What! Timid and confused, you haven't dared

To sustain an interview with a father and a lover?

Ah, madame, could you secretly feel

An unjust repentance over this fatal departure?

IRENE:

Me!

ZOE:

Often the danger whose image we brave

Astonishes courage at the moment of its approach.

Terrified nature and our secret inclinations

Are awakened in us, stronger and more powerful.

IRENE:

No, I haven't changed; I am still the same.

I'm abandoning myself completely to my father who loves me.

It's true, in this fatal moment, I haven't been able

To withstand the looks of a father and a lover.

I couldn't speak, trembling, fainting,

The day refused my obscure sight.

My blood was frozen; without strength and without help

I was reaching the moment that would end my life.

Shall I render thanks to the hands which helped me?

Shall I withstand the life, alas! That they returned to me?

If Leonce appears, I feel my tears spill,

If I see Alexis, I shake and I die.

And I would like to hide from all nature

My feelings, my fear, and the ills I am enduring

Ah! What's Alexis doing?

ZOE:

He intends as sovereign

To place you back on the throne and to give you his hand.

To Leonce, to the pontiff, he's explaining himself as master.

In these distractions I have trouble knowing him.

He won't suffer that you ever dare

To dispose of yourself and leave the palace.

IRENE:

Heaven, you read in my heart, you see my sacrifice,

You will not suffer that I be his accomplice!

ZOE:

How you are in prey to sad battles!

IRENE:

You know them: pity me, don't condemn me.

All that can tempt a weak mortal

To punish herself and to reign over herself

I have done, you know it; I still carry my weeping

To God whose goodness, they say, changes hearts.

He has not harkened to my assiduous complaints

He pushes away my hands extended towards his throne

He distances himself.

ZOE:

And still, free in your sorrows,

You are fleeing your lover.

IRENE:

Perhaps, I cannot.

ZOE:

I see you are resisting the flame that devours you.

IRENE:

By wanting to suffocate it, could I be reigniting it still?

ZOE:

Alexis won't live and reign except for you.

IRENE:

No, Alexis will never be my spouse.

ZOE:

Well, if in Greece a barbarous custom

Contrary to those of Rome, unworthily separates

The widows of Caesars from the rest of mankind,

If this harsh prejudice reigns in our ramparts,

This rigorous law—is it a supreme command

That from the height of his throne was pronounced by God himself?

Against you does he intend to arm himself with his lightning?

IRENE:

Yes: you see what mortal he forbids me to love.

ZOE:

Thus, far from the palace where you were nourished

You are going, beautiful Irene, to inter your life!

IRENE:

I don't know where I am going— Humans, weak humans!

Do we control our fate? Is it in our hands?

(Enter Leonce.)

LEONCE:

Daughter, you must follow me and flee rapidly

This odious abode, fatal to innocence.

Cease to fear and follow on my steps,

The efforts of tyrants that a father doesn't fear.

Against these famous names of Augustus and invincible,

A word, a name from heaven, is a terrible weapon

And religion, which commands them all,

Puts in them a holy bridle that

Brings them to their knees repenting.

My hair shirt, that a prince contemplates with disdain,

Triumphs over his purple, and commands him to the temple.

Your honors, more sure and more constant with me,

Will be independent of flighty humans.

They won't have need to strike the vulgar

With the dazzle borrowed from a foreign pomp.

You've already learned what to disdain;

You are going to reign far from the throne.

IRENE:

I've already told you, I am quitting it without regret.

The new Caesar is coming; I'm leaving and avoiding him.

(She leaves.)

LEONCE:

I won't leave you.

ALEXIS:

(entering) That's too much; stop

For the last time, unjust father, listen.

Hear your master to whom blood binds you

And who has lavished his life for your daughter,

Who has delivered you both from a tyrant,

This unhappy conqueror that you are making desperate.

The sovereign, sacred to the altars of Sophia,

Whose high cabal is tied to yours,

You are seconding against me, and think with impunity

In the name of heaven, to ravish Irene from her lover.

I've served all of you, you, Irene, and Byzantium.

Your daughter was the just reward for it,

The only prize owing to my arm, to my faith

The only object that may be, in the end, worthy of me.

My heart is open to you and you know if I love.

You are coming to carry away from me half of myself.

You who, from the cradle united the two of us

With a paternal hand formed our bonds;

You, by whom she was promised to me so many times,

You are ravishing her from me, when I've conquered her.

After I saved her, and you, and the whole realm!

Too virtuous mortal, you are an ingrate.

You dare to propose that my heart detach itself from her!

Giver her to me, cruel man, or I will tear her from you!

Embrace a tender son, born to cherish you

Or beware an avenger armed to punish you.

LEONCE:

Be neither the one nor the other, and try to be just.

Rapidly carried to this august throne

Deserve your success— Hear me, lord:

I can neither flatter nor fear an emperor.

I didn't leave my profound retreat

To deliver my old age to worldly intrigues

To great passions, to their distracted desires.

I can only announce harsh truths.

Who serves only his God has nothing else to say.

I am speaking to you in his name and in the name of
    the Empire.

You are blind; I must reveal to you

The crime and the dangers you intend to run.

Know that on earth, there's no place,

Or ferocious nation by the world abhorred,

From a clime so savage, where a mortal ever

With such a sacrilege dared to soil the altar.

Hear God who speaks and the earth which screams:

—Your hands have torn the life from your monarch.

Don't marry his widow.— Or, if you dare

To disdain the eternal laws of this voice,

Go rape my daughter and try to please her,

Stained by the blood of a husband and that of a father:

Strike—

ALEXIS:

(turning away) I cannot do it—and despite my wrath

This heart you are piercing is softened for you.

Is the harshness of yours unalterable?

Do you see in me only a culpable enemy?

And will you regret your persecutor

To raise your voice against a liberator?

Tender father of Irene, alas! Be my father;

Relinquish the role of a pitiless judge.

Don't sacrifice your daughter and me

To superstitions whose law you serve;

Don't make an odious and cruel weapon of them.

And don't force them with a paternal hand

Into the unhappy heart that wants to revere you,

And which your virtue is pleased to tear apart.

Such severity is not in nature.

Abandon the imposture of a terrible prejudice—

Cease—

LEONCE:

In what error is your spirit plunging itself?

Is the voice of the universe a prejudice?

ALEXIS:

You argue, Leonce, and as for me, I am sensitive.

LEONCE:

I am like you—heaven is inflexible.

ALEXIS:

You are making it speak, you are forcing me, cruel man

To battle my father and heaven at the same time.

More blood is going to be shed for this unjust Irene

Than shed for Roman ambition.

The hand that saved you can no longer

Do anything but avenge itself.

I will destroy this temple where they dare to outrage me.

I will smash the altar defended by your yourself.

This altar at all times rival of the crown;

This fatal instrument of so many passions,

Loaded by our ancestors with the gold of nations,

Cemented by their blood, surrounded by rapines.

Ingrate, you will see me on these vast ruins

Light the torches of a marriage they reprove

In the midst of debris, of blood, of tombs.

LEONCE:

Now there are the horrors in which supreme grandeur

That is without bridle, is abandoning itself!

I pity you for reigning.

ALEXIS:

I am getting carried away;

I feel it, I blush for it, but your cruelty,

Calm in striking me, studiously barbarous,

Insults with more art, and carries a most rough blow.

Withdraw; flee.

LEONCE:

I will await, lord,

What justice brings me and tells your heart.

ALEXIS:

No, don't wait: decide immediately

If I must avenge myself or if I must die.

LEONCE:

Here's my blood, I tell you, and I am offering it to your blows.

Respect my duty; it is stronger than you are.

(Leonce leaves.)

ALEXIS:

How happy is his fate! Seated on the shore

He looks in pity on this turbulent storm

Which has begun the course of my sad reign.

Irene is the charm and the horror of my life.

Her weakness is sacrificing me to the errors of her father.

To the senseless speeches of a vulgar blind man.

Those in whom I was hoping are all my enemies.

I'm Caesar, I'm in love, and nothing is submissive to me!

What! Without blushing, I can, in fields of carnage

When a Scyth, a German, succumbs to my courage

Over his completely bloody corpse that they bring to my eyes

Carry off his spouse in the sight of the gods

Without a priest, a soldier daring to raise his head!

No one dares to suspect the right of my conquest,

And my fellow citizens will forbid me to love

The widow of a tyrant who wanted to oppress her!

Let's enter. (enter Zoe)

Well, Zoe, what have you come to inform me of?

ZOE:

In her apartment beware of entering.

Leonce and the pontiff are dismaying her heart.

Their holy and funereal voices bring terror to it;

Shivering at their feet, trembling, fainting

Our sad efforts barely recalled her life.

They are daring to snatch her from the walls of this palace.

A sad retreat will forever hide

Abandoned Irene from the rest of the earth.

Such is the destiny of widows of Caesars.

They see in you only a furious tyrant,

A sacrilegious soldier, an enemy of the heavens,

If, wishing to abolish these sinister customs,

You brave the ministers of religion,

The empress in tears, conjures you on her knees

Not to listen to an imprudent wrath

And to allow her to fulfill these deplorable duties

That sacred masters judge inviolable.

ALEXIS:

Masters where I am! I thought not to have any more.

To me, guards, come.

(Enter Memnon and guards.)

My absolute orders

Are that no mortal leave this enclosure

That they be armed everywhere, and that this gate be watched.

Go. They will learn who gives the law

Which of us is Caesar, the pontiff or me.

Dear Zoe, return, inform Irene

That she must obey and that she must bear it in mind.

(to Memnon; Zoe leaves)

Friend, it's with you today, that I am undertaking

To smash in one day all the fetters of tyrants.

Nicephorus is fallen: let's drive out those that remain.

These mental tyrants that my pains detest,

Let Irene's father be arrested in the palace.

Having, in the end, less authority and less audacity;

Let him be distanced from his daughter and reduced to silence.

He shall not raise the populace of Byzantium.

Let this passionate pontiff be guarded in the palace.

Another more submissive to my order is mandated

Who will be more docile to my sovereign voice.

Constantine, Theodosius found them without trouble

More criminal than I in their sad abode.

Their cruelty lacked the excuse of love.

MEMNON:

Caesar, what are you thinking of? This intractable old geezer,

Opinionated, high-born, is still respectable.

He is of those virtues, forced to esteem,

We tremble to oppress even while detesting them.

Eh! Don't you fear by this violence

To do the heart of Irene a mortal offense?

ALEXIS:

No, I've decided on it. I owe it to my grandeur.

And my throne, and my glory—it lacks happiness.

I am succumbing, in reigning, to destiny which outrages me.

Second my distractions, finish your work.

CURTAIN

ACT V

Same as in Act I.

MEMNON:

Yes, sometimes, no question, it is most difficult

To assure for oneself a pure and easy fate

As to find glory in the midst of battle

Which depends less on us than on our soldiers.

I told you: Irene in her just wrath

Will never pardon the outrage on her father.

ALEXIS:

But what! To allow an imperious master near her

Who will reproach her for the power of her eyes,

Who will especially make it a crime to please me

And twisting at his will this simple and sincere heart

Govern her weakness and deceive her candor

Is going to change by degrees her tenderness into horror!

I intend to reign over her as well as over Byzantium.

To cover her with the rays of my total power,

And this proud master, who intends to give her the law

Shall be at the feet of his daughter and serve her with me.

MEMNON:

You are deceiving yourself, Caesar; I've foreseen your alarms.

You've turned your own arms against you.

It's done; I pity you.

ALEXIS:

You've obeyed me?

MEMNON:

With regret; but I've served you.

I seized the old geezer; and Caesar who is sighing

With the weakness of love is teaching me what empire is.

But after this injury, would you have hoped

To draw to you an ulcerated spirit?

Eh! Why consult in such alarms

An old soldier gone white in the horrors of fighting?

ALEXIS:

Ah! Dear and wise friend, how your enlightened eyes

Have indeed foreseen the effect of my distracted desires!

How you know this heart so contrary to itself,

Rebel slave that ruins all it loves;

Blind in its wrath, prompt to contradict itself

Born for passions and to repent them!

(Memnon leaves.)

Come, come, Zoe, you who cherish Irene; (Zoe enters)

Judge if my love has deserved her hate.

If I wished as master, as conqueror, as Caesar,

To display the august Irene chained to my chariot.

I would never order such an odious celebration

At the temple of the Bosporus being prepared with pomp.

I won't insult to this degree these prejudices

That the times implant in the heart of nations.

I intend to prepare this marriage to which I aspire,

Far from an importunate populace attracted by a vain spectacle.

You know the altar raised in these parts

With the simplicity of the hands of our ancestors.

Only admitting for witnesses of the faith that is pledged,

Two friends, a priest, and heaven that forgives.

It's there that before God, I will promise my heart.

Is it unworthy of her? Does it inspire horror?

From pity, tell me if her agitated soul

Recoils in shock from offers that I am making.

If my profound respect can only revolt her:

Finally, if I am offending her in making her reign.

ZOE:

This morning, I admit, in prey to her alarms

Your name spoken made her tears flow.

But since Leonce spoke to you here

Eye fixed, face pale, and mind overwhelmed

She keeps a wild silence with us.

Her heart doesn't make us a sad confidence

Of this powerful remorse which battles her desires.

Her eyes have no more tears, or her voice sighs,

Profoundly struck by her last affront,

By Leonce and you completely occupied,

She has not responded to our urgings

Except with a dying regard and a distracted face;

Unable to repulse from her somber thoughts

The dolorous weight which oppresses her.

ALEXIS:

Alas! She loves you and no doubt fears me.

If in my despair your friendship pities me,

If you can move much in this noble and tender heart,

Decide her at least to see me, to hear me,

Not to reject these humiliated prayers

From an emperor, submissive and trembling at her feet.

The conqueror of Caesar is Irene's slave.

She extends at her choice or shakes off her chain:

Let her say but a single word.

ZOE:

Right in this abode

I see her coming by the secret passage.

ALEXIS:

It's she herself, o heaven!

ZOE:

Attached to the earth

Her view at the sight of us is distracted wildly.

She's hurrying towards us, but without looking at you.

I don't know what horror seems to possess her.

ALEXIS:

Irene, is it really you? What! Far from answering me

She hardly intends to confound me with a look.

(One of the soldiers who is accompanying her brings up a chair.)

IRENE:

(entering) A seat—I'm succumbing— In these isolated parts

Attend me, soldiers.— Alexis, listen. (with an uneven voice, halting but firm more than sad)

Know what I am suffering, and seeing what I dare,

You will grasp the reason for such a conversation,

And it will soon be known if I ought to have spoken

to you.

With a great enough reproach I can overwhelm you,

But the excess of misfortune weakens anger.

Tainted with the blood of a husband,

You are taking a father from me.

You are seeking to raise against you again

This empire and heaven that you are daring to brave.

I see the distraction of your frightful delirium

With that pity that a frenzy inspires.

And I am coming to you only to pull you back

From the depth of the abyss in which I see you entering.

I pity your blind funereal sense

It cannot be cured—a sole role remains to me.

Go seek my father, implore his pardon

Come back with him, perhaps reason,

Duty, friendship, the interest which ties us together,

The voice of blood which speaks from his tenderized

soul,

Will bring closer three hearts which are not in accord.

A moment can end so many sad battles.

Go—bring me the virtuous Leonce;

On my fate with you let his mouth pronounce.

Can I count on it?

ALEXIS:

I am running without examining anything.

Ah! If I dared to think that he could pardon me

I would die at your feet from an excess of joy.

I fly blindly where your order sends me.

I am going to repair everything, yes, despite his rigors,

I intend that with my hand his hand dry your tears.

Irene, believe me, my life is destined

To make you forget this frightful day.

You tenderized father will see in me

Only a tender and submissive son, worthy of your faith.

If in Thrace much blood was shed for you

My outpoured blessings will cover their trace.

If I offended Leonce, he will see the whole realm

Expiate with me this unworthy outrage.

The two of you will reign; my tenderness only aspires

To leave the reigns of empire in his hands.

I am swearing it to the heroes with whom we won the day,

And to heaven that hears me, and you, and my love.

IRENE:

(softening, and holding back her tears)

Go: have pity of this unfortunate.

Heaven tore her from you; for you she was born.

Go, prince.

ALEXIS:

Ah! Great God, witness of my blessings,

I will be worthy yet of my happiness.

IRENE:

Go! (he leaves)

Follow his steps, Zoe, so faithful and dear.

(Zoe leaves.)

IRENE:

(rising)

What have I said? What have I done? And is it what I am hoping?

I no longer know myself— While he was speaking to me

At only the sound of his voice all my heart escaped from me.

Each word, each moment, brought into my wound

Devouring poisons which made nature shiver. (she walks dazed and beside herself)

No, don't obey me, no, my dear Alexis,

Don't bring my father to my obscure eyes.

Return— Ah! I see you:

Ah! I hear you.

Near you I idolize the crime.

O crime! Get away—Heaven! What a frightful object!

What threatening specter is hurling itself between the two of us!

Is it you, Nicephorus! Terrible shade, halt!

Pour out only my blood, strike only my head.

I alone did it all; it's my guilty love,

It's I who betrayed you, who stole life from you.

What! You are joining with him, you my unhappy father!

You pursue this homicidal, adulterous daughter!

Flee, my dear Alexis, turn away with horror

Those eyes so dangerous so powerful to my heart!

Disengage from my hand, your hand reeking with blood.

My father and my spouse are pursuing my lover!

On their embloodied bodies will you make me march

To fly into your arms from those you've torn me?

Ah! I'm coming to myself—Sacred religion,

Duty, nature, honor, to this distracted soul

You are returning her reason, you are calming her spirits.

I no longer hear you, if I see Alexis!

God, that I wish to serve, and that I am still outraging,

Why have you delivered me to this cruel storm?

Against a weak reed why do you want to arm yourself?

What have I done? You know: my whole crime is to love!

Despite my repentance, despite your supreme law,

You see that my lover has won despite yourself.

He reigns, he has conquered you in my obscure feelings.

Well! Behold my heart! That's where Alexis is.

Yes, so long as I breathe he's the sole master of it.

I feel that by adoring him I am going to deny you.

I am betraying marriage, nature, and you—

(Irene draws a dagger and strikes herself. Enter Alexis, Leonce, Memnon, and followers.)

ALEXIS:

I am bringing you a father and I've flattered myself

That we can soften his harsh austerity;

That his justice in the end will find me less culpable.

He will deign— Just heaven! What a horrifying spectacle!

Irene, darling Irene!

LEONCE:

O my daughter! O madness!

ALEXIS:

(throwing himself at Irene's knees)

What demon inspired you?

IRENE:

(to Alexis) My love. (to Leonce) Your honor.

I adored Alexis and I am punishing myself for it.

(Alexis wants to kill himself. Memnon stops him.)

LEONCE:

Ah! My funereal zeal was too barbarous.

IRENE:

(extending her hands)

Remember me—the two of you pity my fate.

Heaven! Take care of Alexis and pardon my death.

ALEXIS:

(on his knees on one side) Irene! Irene! Ah, God!

LEONCE:

(on his knees at the other side of her) Wretched victim!

IRENE:

Pardon, clement God! Is my death a crime?

CURTAIN

VOLTAIRE:

—Her last act being an act of contrition, it is clear that she is saved.—

TANIS AND ZÉLIDE

Translator's Note:

The missing lines in the text, indicated by a row of astesrisks, are also absent in the French original. Voltaire never made the corrections.

CAST OF CHARACTERS

ZÉLIDE, Daughter of the King of Memphis

TANIS, a shepherd

CLEOFIS, a shepherd

PANOPE, Zélide's confidant

OTOES, head of the Magi of Memphis

PHANOR, warrior of Memphis

ISIS and OSIRIS

Shepherds, Shepherdesses, People, Choruses

ACT I

ZÉLIDE:

Beneficent gods, that are adored in these groves,

Continue to protect me from my oppressors!

The Magi of Memphis still pursue me!

And simple shepherds are my only defenders.

It is here that Tanis repulsed the fury

Of our invincible conquerors.

In my cruel misfortune, I have no other pleasures

Than to speak of his courage.

PANOPE:

Have you forgotten Phanor?

ZÉLIDE:

Attached to my father,

He followed my fate; I know his valor.

PANOPE:

Ah! With what indifference you see him!

ZÉLIDE:

He did his duty; my heart is touched by it.

PANOPE:

He braves the wrath of the Magi of Memphis,

Since these tyrants have dethroned the kings,

Since they've shed the blood of your father,

He has risen against them; he has defended your rights;

He has escorted your steps; he loves you: he hopes,

By his exploits, to deserve you.

ZÉLIDE:

Despite all his efforts, wandering, pursued,

I would have perished hereabouts.

He himself was falling under the odious yoke.

We owe to Tanis liberty and life.

How great Tanis is in my eyes!

PANOPE:

Esteem and gratitude

Are the just reward of good deeds;

But could simple shepherds ever

Brave the violence of the tyrants of Memphis?

Your throne is fallen; you have no more friends.

What do you still hope?

ZÉLIDE:

Solely to the arm of Tanis do I owe my deliverance.

I hope all from generous Tanis.

(Shepherds armed with lances enter, with shepherdesses carrying shepherd's crooks and instruments of rustic music.)

CHORUS OF SHEPHERDS:

Stay, reign over our shores;

Know the peace and beauty of life.

Nature has placed in our groves

True virtues unknown in courts.

A SHEPHERDESS:

Without pomp and without envy,

Satisfied with our fate,

We rejoice in life.

We don't fear death.

Innocence and courage,

Friendship, tender love,

Are the glory and the future

Of this fortunate abode.

A SHEPHERD:

It can charm us,

Never defeat us;

We know how to fight.

We know how to love.

CHORUS:

Stay, reign over these shores;

Know the peace and beauty of life.

Nature has placed in our groves

True virtues unknown in courts.

ZÉLIDE:

Herdsmen, happy herdsmen, as sweet as invincible,

You who brave death, you who brave the chains

Of our inflexible pontiffs,

How I love your laughing deserts!

How this abode pleases me! How savage Memphis is!

How have you been able, in these enchanted groves,

Near the walls of Memphis, and near slavery,

To preserve your liberty?

How have you been able to live forever, without masters,

In these peaceable parts?

SHEPHERDS:

We have kept the mores of our ancestors.

We brave tyrants and we love our gods.

ZÉLIDE:

O Heaven! How much grandeur in this simple innocence!

Respectable mortals! Happy heavens! Serene days!

SHEPHERDS:

This is the way all humans once lived.

ZÉLIDE:

But amongst you, Tanis has some power?

SHEPHERDS:

In our happy equality,

Tanis has a gentle authority.

Because his virtues and his valor

Are only too well deserved.

TANIS:

(entering) Is it possible, o God!

Phanor dares to attempt

To expose your beautiful life to our haughty enemies!

What would you go to do?

Alas! On the ramparts of Memphis?

What fate can you expect there?

Our fields, our groves, and our hearts are yours.

Must he bring you to a perfidious people,

That bloodthirsty Magi, a homicidal court,

Carry you away from such sweet favors?

ZÉLIDE:

What! Phanor, after his defeat

By the shores of the Nile, dares to return?

Ah! If I must leave this friendly abode,

Will Tanis wish to abandon me?

TANIS:

We do not ravage the earth.

We defend our fields when they are threatened.

We detest horrid war,

But you are changing our laws since you appeared.

To the ends of the universe, I am ready to follow you.

It wasn't much to help you.

It's because of you that it is sweet to live.

It's by avenging you that it is sweet to die.

(Phanor and his suite enter.)

PHANOR:

The enemy is coming to us, and thinks to surprise us.

It's up to you to second me;

Tanis, and you, shepherds, go: go defend

Your passes that must be guarded.

TANIS:

We have no need of your supreme order.

You have seen us hereabouts

Deliver the princess and save you yourself.

And we know only her eyes as master.

PHANOR:

I am commanding in her name.

TANIS:

Let your pride ponder

Our zeal and our exploits.

Cease to give us orders,

And learn from our example.

PHANOR:

Tanis, in other times, your boldness

Clung to a different language.

TANIS:

And in all times, my courage

Scorns and crushes pride.

ZÉLIDE:

Stop: what distraction are you devising for my eyes?

My fortune is obedient to yours;

All is lost for me if you are not united.

TANIS:

That's enough, pardon, I fly and I obey.

(Exit Tanis and the shepherds.)

PHANOR:

No, I cannot bear

That before my eyes you honor him.

Equality alone offends me.

The injurious preference

Is too odious an affront.

ZÉLIDE:

He's fighting for you yourself:

Is it for you to complain of?

You owe more respect for the exploits of Tanis.

We must treat with caution, we must fear

The great hearts who have served us.

PHANOR:

Go on, finish, ingrate:

Blame on me our common misfortune.

Raise to your level a barbarian, a herdsman.

Forget—

ZÉLIDE:

Do you dare?

PHANOR:

Yes, I see that he prides himself on it.

Yes, you encourage his bold ardor.

Your weakness bursts out,

In your eyes and in your heart.

ZÉLIDE:

Why do you suspect that I am able to descend

To the point of suffering him to live under my rule?

Your threatening suspicions are sufficing to teach me

Who is not unworthy of me.

PHANOR:

O heaven! How right I was to want

To leave this fatal shore today!

Can you outrage my courage to this degree?

ZÉLIDE:

If to equal him to you causes you an outrage,

Surpass his great heart by serving me better than him.

CHORUS OF HERDSMEN:

To Arms! To arms! Let's March! Direct us!

PHANOR:

Well! I am going to perish for your perfidious charms.

I am going to seek death, and I will cherish the blow.

You alone cause my alarms.

I have no enemies more funereal than you. (he leaves)

CHORUS:

To arms! To arms!

Let's march, direct us!

ZÉLIDE:

Ah! I deserve his wrath.

I don't dare confess my secret feelings.

I see, from his distraction,

How much Tanis has known how to please me.

From his new danger, I feel how much I love him.

How much virtue! How much valor!

Gods! For his reward,

Is this greater than my heart?

Must my glory be offended

By such a deserved passion?

No, for his reward,

I owe him all my heart.

CURTAIN

ACT II

CHORUS OF SHEPHERDS:

Victory! Victory!

Our cruel enemies

Have fallen under the blows of generous Tanis.

CHORUS OF SHEPHERDESSES:

Let their memory perish!

Pleasures will no longer be banished.

BOTH CHORUSES:

Triumph! Victory!

THE PRIEST OF ISIS:

Tender Isis, Osiris, first gods of mortals,

Why do you reign only in these happy groves?

Won't you punish further these implacable Magi,

These enemies of your altars?

At the gates of Memphis we brave their power.

But is it enough for us not to succumb?

When will we see them fall

Under the blows of our vengeance?

CHORUS OF SHEPHERDS:

Loveable freedom reigns in these beautiful parts.

What other boons are you demanding of the gods?

CHORUS OF SHEPHERDESSES:

Sweet shepherds, so many fears in these alarms

Are only subdued by our charms.

A SHEPHERDESS:

May these new flowers

Decorate our shepherds.

These to the beauties,

To crown the conquerors.

CHORUS OF SHEPHERDESSES:

Sweet shepherds, so many fears in these alarms

Are only subdued by our charms.

(Dances.)

A SHEPHERDESS:

Of Venus' charming birds,

You are not so faithful.

Of more tender turtledoves,

The raptures are less touching.

The rapid and impetuous eagle,

Carries to the height of the heavens,

With a flight less intrepid,

The shining thunder of the gods.

CHORUS OF SHEPHERDESSES:

Sweet shepherds, so many fears in these alarms

Are only subdued by our charms.

PRIEST OF ISIS:

Come, shepherds, it is time

To consecrate to our gods the noble monuments

Of valor and glory.

CHORUS:

Triumph! Victory!

(They leave. Tanis, and Cleofis remain.)

CLEOFIS:

What! You aren't following their steps?

TANIS:

Remain, don't leave me.

You know my secret flame,

Know the terrible trouble which tears my soul.

CLEOFIS:

Do you suspect Phanor?

TANIS:

In my cruel troubles,

Everything near Zélide alarms me.

Friend, the most proud of mortals

Becomes the most timid lover.

I fear what I adore, I hesitate, I stagger.

My heart speaks to her eyes, my voice dares not speak.

* * * * * * *

In secret, I nourish the flame which devours me.

And when sleep comes to calm my sorrow.

The gods still increase it.

Osiris appeared to me preceded by lightning.

In the breast of profound night,

About him thunder growled.

Neptune raised his waves,

The black abysses have opened.

What have I done to the gods?

What horror threatens!

CLEOFIS:

Osiris is protecting you, he has led your steps.

It's he who has rendered you invincible.

They are warning you, not threatening you.

TANIS:

Osiris, you know how we love.

Isis, in her celestial abode,

Isis alone makes your supreme happiness.

Gods who experience love, favor love!

(As Tanis prays, the gods Isis and Osiris descend in a brilliant cloud.)

ISIS AND OSIRIS:

Love leads you into this barbaric city

Where the Magi rule.

Undergo the terrible fate that Love is preparing for you

And see death without dread.

(They vanish.)

TANIS:

With what new trouble I feel my soul struck!

CLEOFIS:

With what horror I am astonished!

TANIS:

To brave danger and see death without fear,

My heart expected no oracle from Osiris.

But for my tender flames what a funereal omen!

What an oracle for a lover!

O Gods! Of whom Zélide is the image,

Can one displease you by loving her?

(Zélide enters.)

TANIS:

Princess, in my eyes you read my offense.

My crime bursts before you.

I fear celestial vengeance.

But I fear your wrath more.

ZÉLIDE:

I am unaware to what plans your heart is abandoning itself.

In you I see my defender.

If it is a crime, in the depth of your heart,

I feel that mine is pardoning you.

TANIS:

A shepherd adores you and you pardon him!

Ah! I was trembling to say it to you.

I have braved crowned faces,

And their dazzle, and their empire.

My pride deceived me. I listened too much to its voice.

This pride is abasing itself, it begins

From the day I saw you,

To feel that between us there is too much distance.

ZÉLIDE:

There isn't, Tanis: and if there had been,

Love would have made it disappear.

It isn't the grandeurs, which the gods have given birth to in me,

That my heart is most flattered by.

TANIS:

The lover that your heart prefers

Becomes the first of humans.

To see you, to adore you, to please you,

Is the most brilliant of destinies.

But, when you are smiling on me,

Heaven seems enraged.

I would have believed its justice

Always thought like you.

ZÉLIDE:

No, I cannot suspect that heaven doesn't love you.

TANIS:

I've just heard here its supreme oracle.

In Memphis, love must punish me before your eyes.

ZÉLIDE:

Punish you? You, Tanis! What horrible injustice!

Ah! Sooner let Memphis perish!

Let's avoid these odious walls.

Let's avoid this impious and murderous city.

I renounce Memphis, I will dwell hereabouts.

Your laws will be my laws, your gods will be my gods.

Tanis will take the place of nature in its entirety for me.

I will no longer see anything but the two of us.

TANIS AND ZÉLIDE:

May love interest Osiris,

Always loved by Isis and always amorous.

We will be faithful, happy,

In this obscure grove

As you are in the heavens.

PHANOR:

(entering) Cruel, inhuman, Zélide!

* * * * * * *

So this is how I am betrayed!

I did everything for you; love has punished me.

Under the rule of a herdsman, a vile love subdues you!

Ah! If, in your unworthy fetters, you do not fear

The reproaches of the universe,

At least fear that I will avenge myself.

TANIS:

You avenge yourself, and on whom?

ZÉLIDE:

Calm this vain wrath!

I fear neither the universe nor you.

I must confess that I love him.

Do you pretend to force a heart

That depends only on itself?

Are you more my tyrant than my defender?

Ask pardon of Love, it reigns with caprice,

It enchains at its will,

The hearts of shepherds and kings.

For a shepherd like him, I've no need to blush.

PHANOR:

Ah! I blush for you in your blindness.

But you: tremble from the torture which overwhelms me.

You've made the most implacable enemy

Of the most faithful lover.

The asylum wherein they betrayed my faith

Will no longer defend you from my inflexible rage.

We will see if the lover, whose law you submit to,

Will always appear invincible,

As he was in fighting under me.

TANIS:

You can test that, and at this very moment, even.

What finer field for valor.

It is easy to fight under the eyes that one loves.

Don't delay my happiness.

PHANOR:

This is too much and my arm—

ZÉLIDE:

(stopping him) Barbarian that you are,

Rather, pierce this heart full of trouble and ennui.

TANIS:

You deign to stop his indiscreet furors,

Less from fear for me, than from pity for him.

SHEPHERDS' CHORUS:

(entering) Suspend, suspend the inhuman furor,

Which troubles you before our eyes.

Discord and hate

Don't dwell hereabouts.

ZÉLIDE:

Phanor, realize the injustice

Of a barbarous and jealous love.

PHANOR:

If you love Tanis, I must perish;

I am less barbarous than you.

(Phanor leaves.)

CHORUS:

O terrible Discord,

Frightful daughter of tender Love,

Respect this beautiful abode.

Let it be forever peaceful!

TANIS:

Let my furious rival

Vainly exhale his rage.

Zélide is my share.

I will have all the gods for me.

CHORUS:

O terrible Discord,

Frightful daughter of tender Love,

Respect this beautiful abode.

Let it be forever peaceful!

CURTAIN

ACT III

The stage represents the Temple of Isis and Osiris. The statues of these gods are on the altar; they are holding hands to indicate the marriage of these two divinities.

TANIS:

Temple of Isis where nature reigns,

Beautiful place without decorations, image of our customs,

You are going to crown a passion as pure

As our offerings and our hearts.

Neither the love of Phanor, nor the dazzle of grandeur,

Have seduced the beautiful Zélide.

****

Zélide resembles our gods.

For her goodness prefers

The most sincere heart.

The rest of mortals are all the same to her eyes.

Charming moments, delicious moments,

Hasten to embellish this fine day which enlightens me;

Hasten to fulfill my wishes,

Temple of Isis where nature reigns,

Beautiful place without decoration, image of our customs,

You are going to crown a passion as pure

As our offerings and our hearts.

CHORUS OF SHEPHERDS:

Never has Love carried off

A more brilliant victory.

TANIS:

I must await here the beauty who enchants me.

How slow these moments are to my agitated heart.

CHORUS:

Zélide has disdained dazzling grandeur;

Zélide is like us, she is simple and constant:

And her virtues equal her beauty.

GREAT CHORUS:

Never has love carried off

A more brilliant victory.

A SHEPHERD:

In the nearby grove decorated with its attractions,

The pomps of marriage and its joys are preparing.

Our shepherds are trimming her head

With flowers born beneath her footsteps.

Phanor with his friends have left our asylum.

Marriage, tender Love and the Gods, and Peace

Assure us of tranquil days.

(Dances)

In this fortunate retreat,

Drums and fifes,

The scepters of kings, and crosiers,

Are joined in the hands of Love.

A SHEPHERDESS:

Soon, according to the custom established amongst us,

The shepherds consecrated to the gods of our ancestors,

To the sounds of their rustic flutes,

Will bring Zélide to her happy spouse.

TANIS:

Come, fly, dear thing; it's Love that is calling you.

Our runes are traced on young elms.

Time will make them grow, and render them more beautiful,

Without being able to add to my faithful love.

These fields are greener; a new grace

Animates the songs of birds,

Come, fly, dear thing; it's Love that is calling you.

(Enter Cleofis.)

CLEOFIS:

O perfidy! O crime! O eternal sorrow!

TANIS AND CHORUS:

Heavens! What ills are you announcing to us?

CLEOFIS:

Soldiers from Memphis and your jealous rival,

Those who dare not fight against us—

TANIS:

Well?

CLEOFIS:

They have betrayed our simple innocence.

They've carried off Zélide!

TANIS:

O furor! O Vengeance!

CHORUS:

They've carried her off, o gods!

TANIS:

Let's run, let's punish this outrage.

CLEOFIS:

On a vessel hidden near the shore,

They have cleaved the impetuous waves.

Having faith in oaths, we remained calm:

It's the first time they've been betrayed

In the breast of these sweet asylums.

She invoked the gods, she called Tanis:

We didn't respond to her screams,

Except with useless weeping.

TANIS:

Great gods! These are the ills you foretold me.

I will see those unlucky and guilty walls,

Those terrifying Magi whose hands

Shed the blood of wretches.

Friend, it's there I must die.

They could not break you; they dared to betray you.

Let's destroy this impious city.

Friends, it's up to your valor

To punish this perfidy.

Friends, it's up to your valor

To assist my just fury.

CHORUS:

We are going to seek death or vengeance;

We are marching under his standard.

CLEOFIS:

Let's avenge Love, let's avenge Innocence.

But let's fear to arrive too late.

We must cross this inaccessible mountain,

And Memphis, to our eyes, is another universe.

TANIS:

Love sees nothing impossible;

All roads are open to it.

It crosses the earth and the ocean.

It penetrates the breast of hell;

It crosses the boundaries of the world.

Believe the distractions of my outrage.

Memphis will see me dead, or see me avenged.

What do I see? What happy omen?

Our gods are casting the most tender glances on me.

Gods, whose bounty encourages me,

I follow Love and you; everything urges me on, I am going.

CURTAIN

ACT IV

The stage represents the Temple of the Magi in Memphis. To the right and left one sees Pyramids and Obelisks; the capitals of the temple columns are filled with representations of all the monsters of Egypt.

OTOES:

Ministers of my rule that my vengeance directs,

Phanor has made amends for his crime.

May the blood of dangerous partisans of kings,

Which threatened the altar, and that the altar oppressed,

Fall annihilated!

Let's consult our art of formidable secrets;

Let's see by what terrible blows

The guilty are to be confounded,

When sacrilegious pride moves them against us.

CHORUS OF MAGI:

O mighty magic!

Be forever in our hands

The instrument of vengeance.

Make weak humans tremble!

OTOES:

May our impenetrable secrets

Be forever veiled in dark night.

The less they are known, the more they are venerated

By our blind slaves.

CHORUS:

O mighty magic!

Be forever in our hands

The instrument of vengeance.

Make weak humans tremble!

OTOES:

Let's begin our somber mysteries

Hidden from profane mortals;

I am going to pierce the shadows of the fatal future.

And seek eternal decrees of Destiny.

(Terrible symphony)

(They express with a stylized dance the somber horrors of these mysteries)

What do I see? What danger! What horror threatens us!

A shepherd, a simple shepherd,

Is coming to revive the race of kings I have destroyed.

He is erecting a foreign altar.

A vengeful god leads him! A vengeful god hunts us!

CHORUS OF MAGI:

May all armed hell forestall this audacity!

OTOES:

Let's separate all hope from vile sedition

Of kingly blood, of this so funereal blood,

Zélide is the sole remaining.

We must sacrifice her before their eyes.

CHORUS:

Let's be inexorable;

Let's not spare blood.

May beauty, age, and rank

Make us more pitiless.

OTOES:

Let them bring Zélide: all must be prepared

For this terrible sacrifice.

(Phanor enters with his suite.)

PHANOR:

I am come to demand the reward of my service.

You promised it to me, and I must hope for it.

I bring back my followers under your sway.

Zélide is in my hands, our troubles are over.

And Zélide is the unique prize

That I want for my reward.

OTOES:

What are you daring to demand?

PHANOR:

At the foot of your altars,

It's up to you to form this august alliance.

OTOES:

You come to dispute with our immortal gods.

PHANOR:

Heaven! What am I hearing! I tremble, I shiver.

OTOES:

After your criminal conspiracies,

You have much to be pardoned for.

(Otoes reenters the temple with the Magi.)

PHANOR:

O crime! O infernal plan!

I grasp the horrors that this temple is preparing.

It's I, it's my barbarous love,

Which is going to bring the fatal blow.

Avenge me, avenge yourself: prevent the sacrifice

Which is all our destiny.

What do you expect of their justice?

These monsters tainted with blood have never pardoned.

What horrible preparations are revealed to my eyes:

* * * * * * *

Zélide in chains! A sword on the altar!

(Zélide appears at the back of the temple, he continues)

Let's regroup our friends, second my courage,

Share my shame and my rage,

Follow my mortal despair.

(Phanor leaves with his followers.)

ZÉLIDE:

(entering) Get it over with, inflexible monsters.

Strike, cruel minister,

Hasten the vengeance of heaven

With your horrible sacrileges.

What has become of Tanis? Heavens, what do I see?

TANIS:

(running to the altar) Stop, stop, ministers of carnage.

From this bloody temple, I am learning what the law is.

Death must be my share.

Zélide has my heart and my faith.

A husband in these parts can offer himself as victim.

Respect the love that drives me,

Let all your blows fall on me.

ZÉLIDE:

O prodigy of love! O summit of terror.

Tanis sacrificing himself for me!

(to Tanis)

Here is the only moment in my funereal life,

In which I can wish not to belong to you.

(to Magi)

He's not my husband; it's vain that he demands

Rights so dear, a name so sweet.

TANIS:

Ah! Do not betray my hope and my flame!

Let me bear to the grave the happiness of being yours!

ZÉLIDE AND TANIS:

(together)

Save the better half of myself.

Strike, don't wait,

Pardon the one I love.

It's to me that death is owed.

OTOES:

Our unworthy enemy himself declares himself,

He's the one gods and hell have brought here.

TANIS::

I am your enemy, don't doubt it, barbarian.

OTOES:

Let them enchain him,

Let's begin with this sacrifice.

Bold one, you will perish.

But your just death

Won't save her.

Take this sacred sword. Gods! What a frightful prodigy.

This sword falls to pieces, these walls are stained with blood!

Your god vainly imposes on me with this new illusion.

There still remain arrows with which to pierce your breast.

ZÉLIDE:

People, a god takes up his defense.

(Phanor with his followers arrives on stage.)

PHANOR:

Friends, follow my steps, and let's avenge innocence.

OTOES:

(to his Magi) Soldiers who serve me, beat down the insolent.

You, guard these two criminals.

You, march, fight, and avenge the altars.

(The combatants enter into the temple whose gates shut on them.)

TANIS:

O useless prodigy! O dolorous pains!

Phanor fights for you, and I am in chains!

All mine have followed me, but their aid is slow;

I have nothing for you but powerless wishes.

CHORUS:

(behind the scene) Give up, fall, die, sacrilegious offenders.

Our swords are invincible.

ZÉLIDE:

Do you hear the shouts of the combatants?

TANIS:

What harmonious sounds are blending with the uproar of arms!

What an unheard of mixture of sweetness and alarms!

* * * * * * *

(A sweet symphony can be heard.)

CHORUS:

(Behind the scene) Fair gods

Are taking care of your fine lives;

Favorable gods

Are protecting your tender loves.

TANIS:

I recognize the voices of our helpful gods.

These gods of innocence are taking arms for you.

CHORUS OF COMBATANTS:

Fall, tyrants; die sinners.

Fall into the night of death.

ZÉLIDE:

I shiver!

TANIS:

No, fear nothing.

If my gods have spoken, I hope in their clemency.

I believe in their blessings and my heart.

They led my steps into this byway of horror,

They are making their power burst out,

They are extending their vengeful arms.

ZÉLIDE AND TANIS:

Beneficent gods, finish your work;

Deliver the innocent who hope only in you.

Hurl your arrows, crush under your blows,

The barbarism that outrages you.

(The guards lead Zélide and Tanis off.)

ZÉLIDE:

They still fear you, alas! They are separating us.

Death nears, they are separating us.

TANIS:

Let them tremble at the

Voice of heaven which is declaring itself.

It's for us to hope right up to the breast of death.

CURTAIN

ACT V

ZÉLIDE:

Death brings us together here.

The sacrifice is prepared; we will perish together.

TANIS:

Zélide, calm your terrors.

ZÉLIDE:

Our cruel tyrants are conquerors.

Our herdsmen can hardly be seen in the distance

And Phanor has lost his life.

TANIS:

He deserved death; he betrayed you.

ZÉLIDE:

You are alone and disarmed.

And your heart is without fear!

TANIS:

I love you, I am loved.

Love and the gods are my weapons.

ZÉLIDE:

Tanis! My beloved Tanis! Without you, without our loves,

I would brave the death that threatens me.

But these bloody Magi are masters of your life.

We are enchained; you are without succor.

TANIS:

Our chains are going to fall off;

Everything is going to change its face.

ZÉLIDE:

What! The gods will protect us to this degree!

Let's flee these parts—

TANIS:

Me, flee, when I am going to avenge you!

ZÉLIDE:

Don't abuse the celestial favor;

Steal away from these bloody Magi;

All hell is subdued by their funereal power,

Nature obeys their commands.

TANIS:

It obeys mine.

ZÉLIDE:

Heaven! What's this I hear?

TANIS:

From Isis and Osiris, destiny caused my birth.

ZÉLIDE:

Ah! You are of the blood of the gods!

You know that to my eyes

You alone are worthy of being so.

TANIS:

They deigned to test me by the roughest means;

They wanted to recognize me

Only after having made myself worthy of you at last,

When these bloody tyrants

Separated us by a barbaric effort,

I saw my tutelary gods once more.

They revealed to me my glory. They changed my fate.

They've put in my hands thunder and death.

You are going to resume the rank of your ancestors.

Egypt is going to change its gods and its masters.

ZÉLIDE:

Such a great change is worthy of your hands

But I see these inflexible Magi advancing.

Alas! I love you and I fear.

TANIS:

These terrible tyrants will soon be trembling.

OTOES:

People, prostrate yourselves; let the whole earth adore

The eternal judgments of our formidable gods.

Monsters of Egypt, come running—

Recognize my voice, devour

These audacious sinners

With the sword of the vanished altars.

TANIS:

Osiris, my father, strike.

Hurl from the high heavens your ineluctable darts.

(Arrows thrown by invisible hands pierce the monsters which had spread over the stage.)

THE MAGI:

O heaven! Is it conceivable

They can equal our power!

OTOES:

Terrible and holy art, deploy your prodigies.

Confound these new illusions!

Bring from the abysses of hell,

From burning Phelegethon, sparkling flames!

(A whirlwind of flames is seen rising.)

TANIS:

Heavens, open to my voice!

Torrents suspended in the air,

Come and destroy these powerless flames!

(Cascades of water pour from the obelisks of the temple and extinguish the flames.)

CHORUS OF PEOPLE:

O heaven! In this combat which god will conquer?

OTOES:

Dare you doubt? Let the voice of thunder

Growl and decide in my favor!

Lightning, shine alone on the earth,

Elements, make war,

Confound with horror!

TANIS:

The gods have exhausted you, but it's for your torture.

Hear their immediate justice.

Hell is going to succumb, and your power end.

Heaven is inflaming itself, thunder sparks.

Tremble, it's your voice that called it;

It's falling, it's striking, it's punishing you.

CHORUS OF PEOPLE:

Ah! The gods of Tanis are the legitimate gods.

(Thunder falls, the altars of their Magi are overturned.)

TANIS:

Bloody altars, priests laden with crimes,

Be destroyed, be hurled

Into the eternal abyss of

Tenare from whence you came!

(to the shepherds who appear armed on stage)

You, who are coming to avenge Zélide,

Heaven has foreshadowed your hearts and your exploits.

Its justice dwells hereabouts,

It falls only to the gods to reestablish kings

On this bloody debris, on these vast ruins,

Let's celebrate the heavenly favors.

* * * * * * *

CHORUS:

Both of you reign in profound peace.

Always united, always virtuous.

Daughter of kings, child of the gods,

Imitate them, be the love of the world.

TANIS:

Calm succeeds war.

From new heavens, a new earth

Seems formed on this fine day.

On the heels of Virtues, Pleasures are going to appear.

It's all the work of Love.

****

(Dances)

CHORUS:

Both of you reign in profound peace,

Always united, always virtuous.

Daughter of kings, child of the gods,

Imitate them, be the love of the world.

CURTAIN

ABOUT THE TRANSLATOR

Frank J. Morlock has written and translated many plays since retiring from the legal profession in 1992. His translations have also appeared on Project Gutenberg, the Alexandre Dumas Père web page, Literature in the Age of Napoléon, Infinite Artistries.com, and Munsey's (formerly Blackmask). In 2006 he received an award from the North American Jules Verne Society for his translations of Verne's plays. He lives and works in México.

www.ingramcontent.com/pod-product-compliance
Lightning Source LLC
LaVergne TN
LVHW041624070426
835507LV00008B/440